Technology through the Ages

COMMUNICATION
THROUGH THE AGES

From Speech to Smartphones

MICHAEL WOODS AND MARY B. WOODS

TWENTY-FIRST CENTURY BOOKS / MINNEAPOLIS

To Maeve Woods-Powders

Twenty-First Century Books™
An imprint of Lerner Publishing Group, Inc.
241 First Avenue North
Minneapolis, MN 55401 USA

For reading levels and more information, look up this title at www.lernerbooks.com.

Main body text set in Bembo Std Regular.
Typeface provided by Monotype Typography.

Library of Congress Cataloging-in-Publication Data

Names: Woods, Mary B. (Mary Boyle), 1946–author. I Woods, Michael, 1946–author.
Title: Communication through the ages : from speech to smartphones / Mary B. Woods and Michael Woods.
Description: Minneapolis : Twenty–First Century Books , 2024. I Series: Technology through the ages I Includes bibliographical references and index. I Audience: Ages 11–18 I Audience: Grades 7–9 I Summary: "As ancient civilizations formed, people developed spoken and written languages and tools such as paper, the printing press, and more to communicate and disperse information. Discover how early societies created and innovated communication technology"—Provided by publisher.
Identifiers: LCCN 2023032068 (print) I LCCN 2023032069 (ebook) I
   ISBN 9798765610084 (library binding) I ISBN 9798765629901 (paperback) I
   ISBN 9798765638897 (epub)
Subjects: LCSH: Communication—History—Juvenile literature. I Technology— History—Juvenile literature.
Classification: LCC P96.T42 W665 2024 (print) I LCC P96.T42 (ebook) I DDC 302.2— dc23/eng/20231113

LC record available at https://lccn.loc.gov/2023032068
LC ebook record available at https://lccn.loc.gov/2023032069

Manufactured in the United States of America
1 – CG – 7/15/24

CONTENTS

INTRODUCTION

What do you think of when you hear the word *technology*? You probably think of something totally new. You might think of research laboratories filled with computers, microscopes, and other scientific tools. But technology doesn't only refer to brand-new machines and discoveries. Technology is as old as human society.

Technology is the use of knowledge, inventions, and discoveries to make life better. The word *technology* comes from Greek. *Tekhne* means "art" or "craft." Adding the suffix *-logia* meant "the study of arts and crafts." In modern times, the word usually refers to a craft, technique, or tool itself.

There are many types of technology, including medicine, agriculture, and machinery. This book looks at a form of technology that helps make all other technology possible: communication.

Communication is sharing news, ideas, and feelings with other people. It involves speaking, writing, and reading. We also communicate in nonverbal ways such as with smiles or touches. Art and music are also communication. Many forms

4

Modern technology, such as this digital tablet, allows people to create, access, and share information instantly and globally.

of communication require technology. This includes tools such as paper, pens, ink, paintbrushes, and books. Some of the most popular kinds of modern communication, such as direct messaging and television, require electronic tools.

The first humans on Earth moved from place to place, looking for food. Once the earliest humans started communicating, they were able to settle disagreements, work together more effectively, and plan ahead. Around 10,000 BCE, humans began to settle into permanent villages. As villages grew into cities, life became more complicated. People needed reliable ways of keeping records, so they developed writing systems.

Ancient peoples also developed our most basic communication tools. They drew pictures on the walls of caves. They wrote stories, poems, and plays that people still enjoy and study. Some ancient civilizations used smoke signals and even developed postal systems to send and receive mail. New discoveries about ancient communication technology constantly amaze archaeologists.

CHAPTER ONE
Communication Basics

The first *Homo sapiens*, or modern humans, lived about three hundred thousand years ago. They lived in small groups and got their food by hunting game, fishing, and gathering wild plants. When the food in one area was used up, the group moved to a new place. These peoples were hunter-gatherers who made tools from stone, wood, animal bones, plant fibers, and clay.

Our First Words

For a modern person speaking American English, their first words are usually simple, such as *hi* or *no*. But what were the first words or sounds from our prehuman ancestors millions of years ago? They had mouths and throats suited mainly for chewing, swallowing, and breathing. Their larynxes, or voice boxes, were too high in their throats to make a wide range of noises. That changed over thousands of years. The voice box moved lower. Other changes in the brain and skull allowed ancient people to produce sounds needed for complex speech.

Researchers who study the growth of speech face many challenges. The earliest humans did not have writing systems. We have no record of their languages. Researchers also cannot study the speech organs of the first humans, especially the larynx. These organs usually decay and disappear after death.

In 2017 scientists discovered the remains of human jaw and skull bones in northwestern Africa that were about three hundred thousand years old. The bones are similar to those in the heads of modern humans. Discoveries such as this have led scientists to wonder when our human and prehuman ancestors began to talk to one another. Some think it began only about fifty thousand years ago. Others think it happened one hundred fifty thousand years ago or even earlier.

The prehistoric people who drew on the walls of caves seventeen thousand years ago in modern-day Lascaux, France, were pioneers in human communication. Such paintings have been found in caves worldwide.

Talking about Language

One of the most useful tools throughout human history has been language. Even though scientists aren't sure when speech first developed, they know many modern languages share ancient ancestors. Language experts use these ancestors and common features to group languages into families. For example, the romance language family contains languages that come from Latin, such as Spanish and French. And experts have traced Latin to an even earlier, unrecorded language, which scientists call Proto-Indo-European.

Studying languages can help people understand where languages developed and how ancient peoples used them. Spoken language helped people pass on information and share ideas. Ancient peoples worldwide from India to the Americas would also eventually develop oral traditions. They used speech to preserve and pass down stories, cultural knowledge, and history through generations.

Cave Paintings

In 1879 Marcelino Sanz de Sautuola took his daughter, Maria, to explore a cave in Altamira in northern Spain. He had visited the cave before to study animal bones and stone tools. While Sanz de Sautuola worked, Maria wandered farther into the cave. She found a stretch of cave wall covered with colored drawings of bison, horses, and other animals that had not lived in Spain for thousands of years.

Sanz de Sautuola rightly guessed that the cave paintings were from the Paleolithic era. That era began about 2.5 million years ago and ended more than ten thousand years ago. Experts believe the paintings are about fourteen thousand years old. The Altamira caves became world-famous. In the following decades, other explorers also discovered cave art in different parts of the world.

Cave paintings are some of the earliest evidence that prehistoric peoples communicated with symbols and images. Earlier humans probably used only hand gestures or verbal forms of communication that left no traces. But painted or carved symbols were a long-lasting kind of communication.

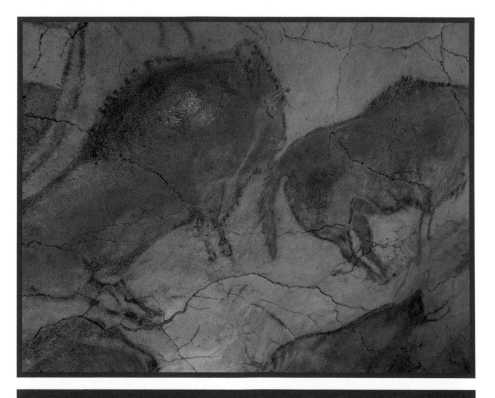

The Sanz de Sautuolas' discovery in 1879 of the Altamira cave paintings in Spain was the first of many similar discoveries. The detailed art, such as the depictions of animals, gave experts new insights into the daily lives of Paleolithic peoples.

Some scientists believe the Chauvet Cave paintings are depictions of current events. One theory suggests that the paintings are the first known recording of a natural disaster that occurred around forty thousand years ago.

Paintings, drawings, and symbols sent the same message to many people. With them, people remembered experiences and recorded them for others.

Some of the oldest known cave paintings come from the Chauvet Cave near the southern French town of Vallon-Pont-d'Arc. It contains more than three hundred paintings, all created between thirty-two thousand and thirty thousand years ago. Many of the paintings include images of bears, lions, horses, and wildcats. Some painters used natural bumps and grooves on cave walls to represent parts of animals' bodies.

Dating Cave Paintings

Archaeologists have several ways of finding out the ages of cave paintings. In some cases, paintings show animals that are extinct, such as woolly rhinoceroses. From studying fossils and other evidence, scientists estimate woolly rhinoceroses died out about fourteen thousand years ago. That means a woolly rhino cave painting is probably older.

Some paintings show animals that no longer live in an area. For example, reindeer used to live in regions of Europe and Asia that eventually became too warm. The reindeer moved farther north. When scientists find a painting of a reindeer in a place where reindeer no longer live, they can guess that the painting was made before the climate changed.

Scientists also date paintings by testing charcoal and other

Magic Paintings

Why did ancient cave painters paint? Maybe they were trying to practice magic. They might have painted scenes of hunters killing mastodons to ask gods or spirits for a successful hunt. Or they might have believed that they could gain a form of control over the animals by painting them. Some scholars have even suggested that the paintings were a way of praying for the survival of a species that hunters relied on for food.

Archaeologists have found hollow animal bones that were used to hold paint. Early peoples may have thought that paint stored in a bone contained the animal's spirit and could bring luck to the hunters.

materials that the artists left inside the caves. Analyzing these materials through carbon dating is often the best way to closely estimate a work's age.

Ancient Finger Painting

The first paintbrush was likely someone's finger. The earliest cave paintings show thick lines of paint. Ancient painters probably dipped their fingers into paint and rubbed them on cave walls. But some lines in cave paintings are too thin to have been made with a finger. Archaeologists think ancient painters made these marks by using sharpened sticks or bird feathers similar to quill pens.

Soot from fires made a deep black paint when mixed with water. Berries and other plant parts made more colors. Some ancient paints were very durable. We can still see the remains of cave paintings done more than thirty thousand years ago.

Cave artists drew with other dry materials such as charcoal, which comes from burned wood. Some ancient artists drew with calcium carbonate, a form of limestone also known as chalk. Chunks of chalk left grayish-white marks on stone.

Engravings

To make the lines, early peoples used a tool called a burin. The burin was a piece of hard rock, such as flint, with a sharp tip. Archaeologists have found worn and broken flint burins on the ground below ancient engravings.

Early artists also created images by chipping away rock to form outlines of images. They probably pressed pointed stones to walls, bones, or other surfaces and tapped them carefully with stone hammers. Artists may have drawn outlines with chalk first. These engravings took a long time to make. Most have been found on flat, horizontal surfaces, where an artist could sit while working.

Some ancient artists combined painting and engraving. The artists began by engraving an outline or image on a rock surface. Then they applied a thin coat of paint that made the engraved lines more visible.

People in Argentina left these painted hands on cave walls more than nine thousand years ago. We know the site of the paintings as the Cueva de las Manos (Cave of the Hands).

13

CHAPTER TWO

The Ancient Middle East

B etween 10,000 and 3500 BCE, some ancient peoples abandoned the hunter-gatherer lifestyle. They began to farm and build permanent villages. Several distinct cultures developed in the Middle East—the region where Asia, Africa, and Europe meet. Sumer is the earliest known civilization. The Sumerians lived between the Tigris and Euphrates Rivers in a region later named Mesopotamia.

Mesopotamia included most of modern Iraq and parts of modern Syria and Turkey. It was home to a series of civilizations, including the Babylonians, Hittites, and Assyrians. These groups were very successful at growing food. For the first time, humans had extra food they could sell to others.

One Technology Leads to Another

As Middle Eastern peoples produced food and goods in greater amounts, government officials had to keep track of laws and who had paid taxes. Farmers needed records of how much

Much of modern Turkey, Syria, and Iraq were part of Mesopotamia.

land they owned and food they had produced. Merchants needed records of the goods they had sold and debts owed to them. The need to keep records led to a new communication technology: writing.

The first known writing was pictographs. Mesopotamian pictographs showed images from everyday life, such as grain, tools, and animals. Pictographs also expressed action, like verbs in modern writing. For example, a picture of a person's mouth combined with a picture of food meant "eat."

15

Clay as Paper

Mesopotamia had lots of high-quality clay. By the fourth millennium BCE, Mesopotamians were making records on small, smooth clay tablets. When a clay tablet was damp, a person could scratch pictures and letters into its surface using a sharpened reed. They then let the clay dry and harden in the sun or baked it in ovens to preserve the writing. Archaeologists have found many tablets from Mesopotamia that are still in good condition.

Some of the earliest known written records come from the Mesopotamian city of Uruk in present-day Iraq.

This Sumerian clay tablet dates to between 3100 and 2900 BCE. The tablet is likely from the city of Uruk and is an administrative record of the distribution of barley.

Uruk, now known as Warka, is one of the first known cities in world history. The city's original walls were built more than five thousand years ago.

Archaeologists have found clay tablets in Uruk dating to between 3300 and 2900 BCE. Most tablets document the trading of food and livestock.

Until the mid-twentieth century, experts wondered if a single person from Uruk, or perhaps a group of merchants, invented writing. But in 1984 archaeologists found clay tablets in present-day Syria that may be older than the Uruk tablets. Because of these findings, most experts believe that many

17

The Dead Sea Scrolls

In 1947 a young shepherd discovered ancient manuscripts in a cave on the northwestern shore of the Dead Sea. They had been hidden there for almost two thousand years. Searches of nearby caves eventually turned up about nine hundred similar manuscripts. Named the Dead Sea Scrolls, they were written between 200 BCE and 68 CE. Many are copies of sections of the Hebrew Bible. Others reveal Jewish religious teachings, customs, and beliefs not discussed in the Hebrew Bible.

Most of the Dead Sea Scrolls are papyrus and leather, but some are etched on copper sheets. The entire collection totals fifteen thousand fragments, many of which are tiny pieces of fragile papyrus.

people invented writing over a long period. The ancient record-keepers from Uruk may have based their writing systems on earlier models that scientists haven't discovered.

Cuneiform

Writing on wet clay was messy. The sharpened tips of reeds created big grooves with raised edges that smeared easily.

Eventually Mesopotamian writers found a better way of recording data on wet clay. They developed simple, linear drawings based on earlier elaborate pictographs. They pressed the lines into clay with special wedge-tipped reed pens. The pens made indentations in the clay with no raised edges.

Cuneiform can be seen on this tablet from the 2000s BCE.

Later peoples named this method of writing cuneiform. Middle Eastern peoples used cuneiform for at least fifteen different languages spanning more than three thousand years.

So Many Symbols

Pictographs worked well as symbols for familiar objects, but they weren't very good for describing new objects or complicated actions. Over time, pictographs slowly became abstract, meaning they no longer looked like the objects they represented. Middle Eastern writers had to memorize the meaning of each symbol—eventually more than two thousand in all.

Around 2800 BCE, people in the Middle East began to use pictures to stand for sounds instead of for objects or ideas. They developed a syllabary. With a syllabary, people could write any word in a language and invent new words.

The First Alphabet?

The symbols that make up an alphabet stand for more specific sounds than the symbols in a syllabary. Researchers don't know for sure what system contained the first alphabet. But many modern languages such as English, Greek, and Russian use alphabets that descend from the Phoenician alphabet.

Archaeologists have found inscriptions on bowls and other utensils in modern-day Palestine made between the sixteenth and thirteenth centuries BCE. The inscriptions belong to a writing system known as Proto-Canaanite. It was developed before Hebrew and other language systems.

Some archaeologists believe the Proto-Canaanite writing

Many Proto-Canaanite symbols look similar to letters in the North Semitic alphabet.

system led to the North Semitic alphabet. Many letters in the North Semitic alphabet resemble Proto-Canaanite pictographs. But they also have more modern features. Peoples of the Middle East used the North Semitic alphabet as early as the eleventh century BCE.

Around the first millennium BCE, the Phoenicians adopted a form of the North Semitic alphabet. They used it to develop a set of twenty-two letters that could be combined to express words. Other cultures later borrowed and adapted letters from the Phoenician system.

Ancient Storytelling

Historians believe ancient peoples first used writing for business and legal records. But soon they began to use it to write stories, entertain, and teach. The ancient Hebrew Bible is one of the most famous written works. Written in Hebrew, it contains many of the teachings of modern-day Judaism. It also contains books of the Old Testament, the first part of the Christian Bible. Among them is the book of Genesis, which describes how God created the world.

We do not know who wrote the Hebrew Bible. Most experts agree that multiple writers were involved over hundreds of years. The Hebrew Bible contains information on the history and people of Israel from the 1300s BCE to the 100s BCE. Different sections feature different styles of writing.

The oldest known written story is the *Epic of Gilgamesh*. At first, Mesopotamian storytellers told the tale of Gilgamesh from memory. Later storytellers wrote it down on clay tablets as early as 2000 BCE. But beginning around 500 BCE many of these tablets were lost, broken into fragments, or buried. The texts were missing for almost two thousand years. That changed in 1853 when archaeologists found clay tablets with much of the epic.

An ancient relief carving from the ninth century BCE, found in modern-day Syria, shows a scene from the *Epic of Gilgamesh*. Gilgamesh is in the center, between two bull men.

CHAPTER THREE
Ancient Egypt

A round 8000 BCE, northern Africa's wet climate became drier. Hunter-gatherers in the area began to move east, toward the Nile River in Egypt. By about 7000 BCE, people had built permanent settlements along the river. The Nile flooded its banks every midsummer. The floodwater soaked the soil and deposited fertile, mudlike silt on land.

Many plants grew along the shores of the Nile. Early Egyptian farmers raised wheat, barley, vegetables, and fruits. The papyrus plant also thrived there.

Paper from Papyrus

Papyrus grows in creeks and rivers, sometimes as tall as 15 feet (4.6 m) high. The reed-like plant has a triangular stem that may be more than 2 inches (5 cm) wide. Ancient Egyptians turned these stems into an early form of paper.

Papermakers cut the stems into strips and scraped away the inner layers of fiber. They placed several strips side by side to form a long, narrow rectangle. They spread shorter

The yearly flooding of Egypt's Nile River made nearby soil suitable for growing grains, fruits, and plants such as papyrus. Papyrus was used to make ancient paper.

strips on top of those. Next, the papermakers wet the strips, beat them with hammers, and pressed them under heavy weights. The pressure sealed the two layers together. Papermakers left the sheets to dry and then polished them. The resulting sheets were bright white and smooth.

Papermakers often glued together up to twenty sheets to

"The nature of papyrus too is to be recounted, for on its use as rolls human civilization depends, at the most for its life, and certainly for its memory."

—Pliny the Elder, Roman philosopher and politician, *Naturalis Historia*, 706 CE

25

This papyrus illustration depicts figures from Egyptian mythology.

create rolls more than 30 feet (9 m) in length. When the rolls were made correctly, the seams between the pages were almost invisible.

The earliest known example of paper made from papyrus dates to around 3100 BCE. Archaeologists discovered this papyrus in an Egyptian tomb. Papyrus papermaking spread to Greece by the sixth or seventh century BCE and then to Rome.

Sacred Carvings

Many people think of Egyptian hieroglyphics, a system of picture writing, when someone mentions ancient writing.

Egyptian hieroglyphics used two main kinds of symbols—ideograms and phonograms. Ideograms are pictures that represent a specific object or idea. Phonograms are pictures that stand for specific sounds. Some represent a single sound. Others represent the combination of two or more sounds. Using ideograms and phonograms together, Egyptian writers could express many ideas in detail.

Beginning around 3000 BCE, Egyptians mainly used hieroglyphics for religious inscriptions on monuments and temples. Later, merchants and politicians also used hieroglyphics. Trained writers called scribes wrote the symbols on papyrus using ink or carved them on stones.

From the Greek word *hieroglyphikos*, meaning "sacred carving," hieroglyphics have been discovered carved into temple and tomb walls and written on papyrus. The writing was complicated and meant for royals and priests, so most Egyptians could not read the text.

27

The hieratic system was simpler than hieroglyphics and better suited for writing longer works.

At first the hieroglyphic system had around eight hundred different symbols. By 300 BCE the number increased to more than six thousand. Scribes wrote in hieroglyphics from top to bottom. But hieroglyphs could be written from left to right or right to left. Readers had to pay attention to the direction hieroglyphs faced to understand a message.

Other Ways of Writing

Egyptians developed hieratic writing around the same time as the hieroglyphic system. Hieratic symbols often look like simplified hieroglyphics. The hieratic system included fewer symbols than the hieroglyphic system. Archaeologists have found some samples of hieratic religious writing, but many of the documents they've discovered are personal letters or business records.

Hieratic writing is a form of cursive—the end of one letter usually connects to the following letter. A scribe using hieratic writing could work quickly, writing a line without lifting their pen.

Around 700 BCE, Egyptian scribes developed demotic writing. Demotic writing looks much like simplified hieratic writing. Scribes could write with this system even faster. Both systems were written from left to right and top to bottom. Scribes used the demotic system for letter-writing and recordkeeping.

The Life of a Scribe

Some scholars estimate that fewer than 5 percent of ancient Egyptians knew how to read or write. So, scribes were

A wall painting in the Tomb of Menna features the Egyptian god Thoth. He was known as the patron of scribes and a god of the moon, learning, and writing.

admired and had some of the best jobs. Rulers made many people do hard, dangerous work, such as building pyramids. But scribes worked in clean, safe conditions, usually in palaces.

Merchants, religious leaders, and government officials all depended on scribes. Scribes wrote down laws and maintained records. They copied old documents and helped explain religious rules.

To become a scribe, a person had to know how to read, write, and do math. A scribe usually went to school and then worked with experienced scribes for a period of years to perfect their skills. Scribes had to master hieroglyphic, hieratic, and demotic writing. In 332 BCE, Greece conquered Egypt. Afterward, scribes also had to learn Greek forms of writing, so they could work for their new rulers.

Limestone Scrap Paper

Between 1550 and 1100 BCE, Egyptians buried royalty in a special cemetery called the Valley of the Kings. Scribes, artists, painters, and other skilled craftspeople decorated the tombs of rulers buried there. These craftspeople lived in a town near the Valley of the Kings called Deir el-Medina.

An unusually large number of the men of Deir el-Medina were literate—around 40 percent at times. For scrap paper, the men used flakes of limestone called ostraca. They made scratches on the stone with sharp tools. Deir el-Medina was buried under desert sands three thousand years ago. Archaeologists digging at the site have found thousands of ostraca containing notes, receipts for deliveries, and even love songs.

Deir el-Medina was home to many craftspeople and other workers.

CHAPTER FOUR
Ancient India

The Sanskrit language arrived in ancient India as early as 1700 BCE. Many scholars believe that a group of people from Central Asia, the Aryans, brought it when they invaded and settled in modern-day northern India. The Aryans were probably named for their language. Sanskrit is an Indo-Aryan language, branching from the Indo-European language family. Other scholars believe the Aryans came from India and were named for their social status. *Arya* may have referred literally to nobility in ancient Sanskrit.

Sanskrit spread throughout India over several hundred years. Indian writers used Sanskrit to write about religious rituals and to retell myths and legends. Birch bark and dried palm leaves were the most popular materials to write on. Ancient peoples wrote on them with quill or reed pens using ink made from plants.

Unlike some other ancient languages, Sanskrit was written in many different regional writing systems, such as the Śāradā system in northern India and Gujarātī in the west. But the Devanāgarī system became popular in the 700s CE.

The Indus River Valley in modern-day India, Pakistan, and Afghanistan was home to a technologically advanced civilization known for its inventions, architecture, and written language.

The system is a combination of a syllabary and an alphabet. People still use it to write in many Indian languages, including Sanskrit.

Sanskrit Lit

Historians divide ancient Indian literature into three stages. They are the Vedic period, the epic period, and the classical period. The first stage of Sanskrit literature, the Vedic period, lasted from about 1500 to 200 BCE. During this time, priests began to record prayers, religious songs, and instructions that had been passed down orally. Their writings make up four books called the Vedas.

The earliest of the books, the *Rigveda*, dates to around 1400 BCE. The *Rigveda* contains more than one thousand hymns. Indian writers later composed the *Samaveda*, *Yajurveda*, and *Atharvaveda*. These books also contained religious poems and mantras.

The epic period happened around 600 to 100 BCE. It marked the writing of two famous Sanskrit epic poems, the *Ramayana* and the *Mahabharata*. The *Ramayana* tells the story of Rama, a prince who saves his wife from a powerful

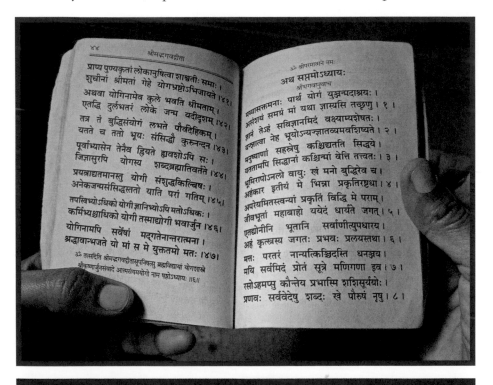

Ancient Indians wrote important religious texts in Sanskrit. Although most people don't speak Sanskrit anymore, some Hindu priests use it in religious ceremonies.

COMMUNICATION THROUGH THE AGES

demon. The *Mahabharata* tells the story of a family divided by a war between two kingdoms. The poet Valmiki is said to have written the *Ramayana*, and the poet Vyasa the *Mahabharata*. But many historians don't believe that either poem had a single author. Indian peoples probably told the epics orally before they were written down.

The classical period lasted from about 500 BCE to 1000 CE. Historians associate the start of this period with the life of Pāṇini, who was most likely born in Śalatura in northwest India in the 500s BCE. Pāṇini wrote *Ashtadhyayi*, a guide to Sanskrit grammar.

As with all languages, Sanskrit changed over time. The Sanskrit that people spoke at the beginning of the Vedic period would probably have sounded strange to people at the beginning of the classical period. Pāṇini's guide provided more than four thousand rules for the Sanskrit language over eight chapters. Pāṇini was not the first person to study grammar. But he was the first to write such a detailed guide to it.

Ashoka Says

Around 324 BCE Chandragupta Maurya started the Mauryan empire, which controlled most of India for more than one hundred years. Chandragupta's grandson Ashoka ruled India from about 273 to 232 BCE. Ashoka developed one of the world's earliest and best road-sign systems.

Road signs are an example of mass communication. They send messages to many people at once. Emperor Ashoka ordered that stone pillars be posted along the Royal Road, a 1,700-mile-long (2,736 km) trade route that ran from the

The Tale of Ten Princes

In the sixth or seventh century, the Indian writer Daṇḍin wrote *Dashakumaracharita*. The book describes the marriages and adventures of ten princes. Some scholars think of it as one of the world's first novels.

Unlike the authors of earlier works such as the *Ramayana*, Daṇḍin chose not to tell his story in verse but instead in prose, which is more like spoken language. Works of prose do not keep to a line-by-line structure like most poems. While many poems feature rhyming lines or a steady rhythm, most prose works do not.

Middle Eastern city of Susa (in present-day Iran) to northern India. The huge pillars provided travelers with directions and featured advice from Ashoka. He urged travelers to obey laws and be good citizens.

CHAPTER FIVE

Ancient China

The earliest Chinese society we know of emerged between 5000 and 3000 BCE in the Yellow River valley of northern China. These early peoples settled into farming before inventing some of the most important writing tools in history. They invented paper and developed printing techniques.

No Alphabet Needed

The earliest known examples of Chinese writing date to the eighteenth century BCE. Archaeologists have found pictographs carved on pieces of bone and tortoiseshell.

As the Chinese writing system evolved, Chinese writers developed a logographic system. In logographic writing, symbols stand for words or parts of words rather than the sounds used to make those words. By around 1400 BCE the Chinese writing system included more than two thousand commonly used symbols.

This piece of silk features a poem by Emperor Lizong. He ruled in China from 1224 to 1264 CE.

Tapa Books

The Chinese made books centuries before the invention of paper. By 3000 BCE writers were using a strong, flexible material called tapa. People made tapa from the inner bark of mulberry, fig, or laurel trees. They dried and pounded the bark until it was smooth.

To make a book, they cut holes in sheets of tapa and tied the sheets together with string. These books didn't last very long. The pages tended to crack and rot. Books were also not common. Tapa was expensive and difficult to make.

The Chinese also wrote on silk made from the cocoons of silkworms. But silk was expensive. Only the richest people could afford it.

Chinese Ink Sticks

The Chinese made their first inks from berries, tree bark, and other natural substances. Many plants contain tannins. These

A traditional set of Chinese writing instruments includes an ink stick, an ink slab for mixing the ink with water, and brushes for writing.

chemicals can give a pale yellow or light brown color to paper and other materials. Early Chinese inkmakers used tannin from tea leaves and other plants.

Historians believe Tien-Tchen developed Chinese ink, also known as India ink, between 2600 and 2500 BCE. Chinese ink is one of the finest inks used for writing and illustration. To make it, early Chinese inkmakers used carbon black, a sooty material produced by burning tar, pitch, or bone.

Chinese ink was not liquid. It came in solid sticks. Inkmakers mixed carbon black with glues or gums and molded the ink into cakes or sticks. To write with Chinese ink, a person placed an ink stick in water before moving it across a surface.

Fear of Books

Between the fifth century and the third century BCE, China was made up of small warring states. By 221 BCE the ruler Qin Shi Huang had unified all the rival states into a single powerful nation.

When Qin Shi Huang took power, people in different regions used different characters to stand for the same words. People in one area often couldn't understand the writing of people in another. The emperor believed a united people needed a shared writing system and wanted to make sure that everyone understood his orders. He ordered everyone to use the same set of about three thousand pictographs. This system is still in use in China.

In 213 BCE Qin Shi Huang ordered all books in China be burned, except those dealing with medicine, agriculture,

Confucius

The philosopher Kong Qiu is one of China's most famous writers. He lived from 551 to 479 BCE. Most people know him as Confucius.

Confucius encouraged people to live honest lives and to treat others in an ethical way. He believed that people learn best through public service and interaction with others. During his lifetime, he was not well known outside his province. But his followers wrote down his teachings in a book called *The Analects*.

After his death, his advice spread throughout ancient China. Most of it was practical. One of his proverbs was, "Set your heart upon the Way; rely upon moral power; follow goodness; enjoy the arts."

the history of the Qin state, and a few other topics. He believed books written before the new writing system developed would hold back China's progress. Many people refused to comply with the order. Many old books survived, but the emperor had scholars executed for owning and preserving them.

Real Paper

The Han dynasty ruled China from 206 BCE to 200 CE. This period produced one of our most basic communication tools: paper.

Cai Lun, a member of the royal court, is traditionally

41

credited with inventing paper. In about 105 CE he developed paper made from mulberry tree bark, old rags, fish nets, and crushed bamboo. The material was strong but flexible and easier to make than tapa. Cai Lun's apprentice, Zuo Bo, helped improve the process even more, and the method quickly spread throughout China.

Chinese papermakers usually soaked bark and bamboo in water until they became very soft. They separated the fibers by beating and stirring them in water. This process resulted in a thick mixture called pulp. Papermakers spread the pulp on a screen equal to the desired size of the piece of paper. When dry, the pulp stuck together to form a single sheet.

火足楻煮

Ancient Chinese papermakers followed Cai Lun's method for hundreds of years. In this image of an eighteenth-century woodcut illustration, a papermaker cooks bamboo stems to soften them.

Spreading the Word

Around the same time Cai Lun developed paper, Chinese clothmakers began block printing pictures and designs on fabric. We still use this technique.

To make block prints, clothmakers carved raised words or designs on wooden blocks. They put ink on the raised images and pressed the blocks onto sheets of fabric. Chinese printmakers soon used the same technique to transfer writing onto paper.

Printing made it faster and less expensive to produce books and copies of documents. Before printing, scribes often needed weeks or months to hand-copy a single book. That time and effort made books very expensive. Only kings, emperors, and other wealthy people could afford them. Printing made books and reading available to more people.

But block printing was still expensive. Each page of a book needed its own carved block. In the eleventh century CE the Chinese improved printing even more by inventing a movable type. This consisted of small clay blocks, each stamped with one letter or symbol. Since each letter was separate, the blocks could be arranged to form any word and reused for different books.

CHAPTER SIX
The Ancient Americas

The first people in North America probably arrived more than twenty thousand years ago. They came from Siberia in modern-day Russia. One theory proposes that humans crossed a land bridge connecting Siberia and modern-day Alaska when ocean levels were lower. Another theory claims ancient peoples sailed from Siberia, keeping close to the coast of the Pacific Ocean and camping on shore to rest and get fresh water. No matter how they reached North America, these peoples were hunter-gatherers and probably followed herds of animals farther into the continent.

Ancient Americans slowly moved south through modern-day Canada to the American Great Plains, modern-day Mexico, and Central America. Scientists once believed people reached the tip of South America about twelve thousand years ago. But new evidence suggests it happened more than fourteen thousand years ago.

Many ancient Indigenous nations had oral traditions. They relied upon the spoken word to share information and preserve their cultures. People told children legends

Historians believe more than one thousand Indigenous civilizations lived in what is now the United States. Each group had its own language and method of communication, many of which included both spoken words and gestures.

about the start of the world or tales of great heroes and passed down knowledge about their people's history and the natural world. These stories moved across generations through voice, memory, and imagination. But the early peoples of North and South America also devised other communication technologies.

Hand Talk

The beliefs and practices of Indigenous nations were very

45

different throughout the ancient Americas. So were their languages. Historians believe that Indigenous peoples who lived north of present-day Mexico spoke about three hundred different languages alone. Some of these languages were similar. But conversation among people of different nations was often impossible.

Sometimes multiple cultures shared a trade language, which they all spoke when exchanging food or goods. This language was usually similar to the native language of a group that lived in a high-trade area. Chinook Wawa was one example. The Chinook peoples lived near the Columbia River in modern-day Oregon, Washington, and Canada. They traded with other nearby groups. Over time, many

A Sioux man (*right*) demonstrates Hand Talk.

Totem Poles

Indigenous peoples of the northwestern United States and Canada created colorful carved wooden posts known as totem poles. Totem poles featured pictographs representing animals, spirits, and community members.

Northwestern nations placed welcoming poles to greet and guide people. The Haida peoples built mortuary poles. They were grave markers honoring the dead. A box at the top held remains of the dead body. When a house changed hands, some cultures built memorial poles to honor the past owner and identify the new one. Many poles recorded history, such as important events or the history of a particular individual, family, or nation.

Some totem poles represent the myths and legends significant to a family. Others were created to either welcome or scare away strangers, or to celebrate a special occasion.

Smoke Talk

Ancient Indigenous Americans were among the many peoples who used smoke signals to communicate over long distances. The technology was simple but brilliant. The signaler built a smokey fire. Then they covered it with a wet blanket or hide. The wet cover trapped smoke, and then the signaler yanked off the cover to release puffs of smoke. Indigenous peoples used codes to communicate in this way. Different nations developed different codes. A certain number of smoke puffs might warn people of danger, call them to a meeting, or deliver news.

traders adopted Chinook Wawa, which was partly related to the Chinook language.

Ancient Great Plains peoples such as the Cheyenne and the Comanche took a different approach. Rather than a shared verbal language, they developed a way to communicate with hand gestures. It's called Plains Indian Sign Language or Hand Talk.

Nobody knows when these peoples first used sign language. In the 1800s, white settlers were pushing eastern Indigenous Americans toward the west. Hand Talk continued to develop as new groups were forced to share the same areas. Some peoples of Plains cultures still use it.

Mesoamerican Writers

Researchers have found examples of early writing from several different cultures in present-day Mexico and Central

America. Historians use the term Mesoamerica to describe this area and its cultures prior to the arrival of European explorers in the 1500s.

One was the Olmec culture. The Olmecs lived in southern Mexico between 1200 and 400 BCE. Historians believe they were the first American peoples to develop a calendar and use a zero in math. An accidental discovery in the late 1990s suggests they were the first to write too. Road builders stumbled on a stone tablet in a pile of debris. Carving on the tablet turned out to be the first known writing in the

Many Mesoamerican cultures used a sacred calendar called a tonalpohualli that followed a 260-day cycle. The calendar in this picture is from the Aztecs. But the Olmecs were probably the first to develop and use a tonalpohualli.

Americas. Called the Cascajal Block, the tablet dates from around 900 BCE. It contains more than sixty symbols, some of which look like plants, animals, or insects.

Before the discovery of the Cascajal Block, most scientists thought the Zapotec were the first society in the ancient Americas to write. The Zapotec society emerged a few centuries after Olmec society in Oaxaca in present-day southern Mexico. The oldest known example of Zapotec writing comes from a Zapotec monument called Monument 3. Its stone surface shows a drawing of a dead or injured person. Two pictographs are drawn between their legs. They may be the person's name. Monument 3 dates from between 600 and 500 BCE.

Maya Writing

The Maya emerged around 2500 BCE. They developed a powerful empire in modern-day southern Mexico, Guatemala, Belize, El Salvador, and Honduras. Sometime around 300 BCE they invented one of the most advanced writing systems in the ancient Americas.

Maya writing is similar to Egyptian hieroglyphic writing. It consists of more than seven hundred pictographs, including faces, animals, and other objects. Each symbol carries one or more meanings. Writers combined pictographs to form words or ideas. They drew pictographs inside small squares and arranged the squares into columns. Maya writing moves from left to right and top to bottom.

The Maya wrote books, painted inscriptions on pottery, and carved words into stone monuments. Archaeologists have

Maya pictographs, such as the ones seen here, often feature images of people or animals.

found many inscriptions on rectangular slabs of stone set upright like signs. They have decoded many Maya symbols. But understanding whole phrases or stories is difficult and confusing. One symbol can represent several ideas.

The ancient Maya wrote on long sheets of bark from fig trees. Some sheets were more than 20 feet (6 m) long. Maya writers covered the sheets with white paint. Priests

This page from a Maya codex demonstrates ancient Maya pictographs. Created around the eleventh century CE, the full codex contains information about astronomy, religion, weather, medicine, and more.

and scribes wrote glyphs on the sheets with thin brushes and ink made from soot. They folded each sheet into pleats to make a kind of book called a codex. Codices contained calendars, astronomical tables, and information about religious ceremonies.

Maya Libraries

Archaeologists believe the Maya stored codices in big libraries. Literate Maya were typically priests or rulers, and the libraries were most likely collected within large temples. Many of the books rotted over time in the hot, wet rain forest climate.

In 1519 Spanish explorers landed in Mexico. They discovered Maya books. Spanish priests tried to convert the Maya to Christianity. On July 12, 1562, a group of Spanish priests punished people who would not convert by burning about five thousand Maya religious images and more than twenty books.

Only three of those books still exist. The lack of surviving books makes it difficult for modern people to understand ancient Maya communication technology.

Knot Writing

The Inca had a vast empire along the western coast of South America in the 1200s to 1500s. Centered in the Andes mountains, it included parts of present-day Colombia, Ecuador, Peru, Chile, Bolivia, and Argentina. The Inca recorded numbers and information on rope-like devices called quipus. Quipus consisted of strings made from cotton or animal hair twisted into knots. The order of the knotted strings hanging from a rope encoded numbers and information. Knots stood for different numerical amounts, usually in amounts of ten. The Inca occasionally used color-coded strings as well.

Rulers and merchants used quipus to communicate with distant parts of their empire. They knotted messages on quipus, and a runner delivered them. Government officials and village leaders also stored quipus like modern people store files in computers.

Spanish conquistadors destroyed many Incan quipus in the 1500s. The Spanish feared the Inca were using quipus to spread dangerous messages. But modern-day researchers have been able to find and preserve several hundred ancient quipus.

CHAPTER SEVEN
Ancient Greece

The Greeks wrote plays, histories, poems, and speeches that people still read and enjoy. Few ancient people actually read these works. Instead, actors and public speakers memorized the works and recited them to audiences. The Greeks passed some stories and poems down through generations without writing them down. Most people had little need for written communication. Writing was important mainly for government officials who kept track of laws and taxes, and for merchants, who kept business records.

Written communication became more important as Greece became more involved with other countries. The Greek military leader Alexander the Great, who lived from 356 to 323 BCE, conquered many surrounding countries, including Egypt. As Greek culture and trade expanded, writing helped people preserve knowledge and track new information. It also allowed them to communicate over long distances in letters.

The Greeks performed famous comedies and dramas in the Odeon of Herodes Atticus theater. Located on the Acropolis in Athens, Greece, the theater was built between 160 and 174 CE.

Borrowing an Alphabet

For years, Greek merchants regularly traded with the Phoenicians. They grew familiar with the Phoenician alphabet. Around the eighth century BCE, the Greeks began to use it to write their own language. They borrowed nineteen of the Phoenicians' twenty-two letters. They also added a few new letters, including phi (φ) and psi (Ψ), to represent sounds missing from the Phoenician alphabet. Although the Greeks kept the Phoenician symbols, they changed many pronunciations. The Phoenician symbol *aleph* (A or α) became "alpha," the first letter of the Greek alphabet. The symbol *beth* (B or β) became "beta," the second letter.

At first the Greeks wrote like the Phoenicians, from right

The ancient Greeks' writing system (*left*) was patterned on the Phoenician alphabet (*right*).

to left. But writers sometimes flipped letters around so they faced in the opposite direction. They then adopted a new style. They alternated writing one line right to left and the next left to right. By 500 BCE, the Greeks wrote from left to right only. They adopted a standard twenty-four-letter alphabet around 400 BCE.

Books without Pages

The ancient Greeks borrowed papermaking technology from ancient Egypt. Greek writers were mentioning papyrus by the fifth century BCE. More than thirty thousand Greek papyrus scrolls have survived. The oldest date to the fourth century BCE.

The Greeks wanted to fit as much information as possible on each scroll. They wrote in columns about 3 inches (8 cm) wide, with thin spaces between columns and margins on each side of the page. Few surviving scrolls include art except practical images such as diagrams.

Greek scrolls rarely exceed 35 feet (11 m) in length. Rolled up, a typical scroll measured between 1 and 1.5 inches (2.5 and 4 cm) thick. Scrolls were about 9 or 10 inches (23 or 25 cm) high. People unrolled the scrolls to read them, usually unrolling with the right hand while rewinding with the left. Some scrolls wrapped around a wooden roller.

From Epic Poems to Prose

Around the 700s BCE, the poet Homer wrote two famous epic poems, the Iliad and the Odyssey. The Iliad tells the legend of the Trojan War, which supposedly took place in the twelfth or thirteenth century BCE. The Odyssey tells the story of Odysseus, a hero struggling to return home after the Trojan War. Homer based his poems on stories the Greeks had preserved through centuries of oral storytelling.

Drama as an art form flourished in Greece in the

Ancient Direct Messaging

Around 500 BCE, the Greeks designed a system to quickly send messages from one city to another. They built a series of towers between major cities. Each tower could be easily seen from the next. Holes at the tops of the towers represented letters in the Greek alphabet. By lighting fires in the right holes, Greeks could send simple messages, such as "danger."

500s BCE. By the 400s BCE, Greek people flocked to see plays, such as those Sophocles wrote. Sophocles's plays often ended tragically and featured powerful moral lessons. His work *Oedipus Rex* tells the story of a ruler, Oedipus, who seeks the murderer of a man whom he himself unknowingly killed. Unlike most modern playwrights, Sophocles and his fellow writers wrote in verse.

Around the 400s BCE, public speaking became a common way to present ideas among politicians and thinkers. This form of speaking is called rhetoric. A group of teachers and writers called Sophists worked to determine the best ways to present rhetorical arguments.

Building Collections

Upon conquering Egypt in 332 BCE, Alexander the Great founded Alexandria on Egypt's northern coast. Alexandria became home to the most famous ancient library.

General Ptolemy Soter ruled Egypt from 323 to 285 BCE. Ptolemy and his adviser Demetrius of Phaleron began building a great library. Many scholars believe Ptolemy II finished the project after his father's death. The library of Alexandria was one of the largest in the ancient world. It may have held between forty thousand and seven hundred thousand scrolls.

Battle for the Biggest

Written records became so important in Greece that rulers Ptolemy V and Eumenes II almost went to war over them. According to legend, Ptolemy V wanted the Alexandria library to remain the largest in the world. Eumenes founded his own library in Pergamum in modern-day Turkey. Eumenes also wanted to have the world's largest library.

Ptolemy banned the shipment of papyrus from Egypt to Pergamum. Eumenes needed a new substance for recording words on paper. Around 190 BCE, craftspeople in Pergamum developed parchment. Parchment is a heavy, paperlike material made from animal skins.

Other people had written on animal skins before. Records show the Egyptians used leather as a writing surface about 2450 BCE. Mesopotamian scribes may have also used it. But leather rotted easily. People could only write on one side. Parchment was double-sided and lasted much longer than paper. Some surviving parchment books were written more than one thousand years ago.

To produce parchment, workers removed the hair and flesh from a hide. They stretched the skin tightly in wooden frames. Workers treated the skin with chalk to make it brighter. Then they rubbed the skin with pumice to make it smooth.

Even after the introduction of parchment, many people still used papyrus scrolls. Parchment did not become the ancient world's main writing material until around the fourth century CE. The codex was also replacing the scroll around this time. Codices were formed by folding papyrus or parchment into smaller sheets and sometimes stitching multiple sets of sheets together. Parchment was more popular for codices. It was stronger and could be folded more. Sheets were bound together along the side, much like modern books. A parchment codex was easier to page through, write on, and carry than a papyrus scroll.

CHAPTER EIGHT
Ancient Rome

The Ancient Latins formed villages in present-day central Italy around the 1000s BCE. One village grew into the city of Rome. The people there became known as the Romans. Over centuries, the Romans conquered other lands in Italy and throughout much of Europe. They made many advances in communication technology. The language Latin and the Roman style of writing were two of their most important contributions to the history of communication.

The first traces of Latin writing appear in inscriptions dating from the 600s BCE. The Romans based the Latin alphabet on that of the Etruscans, who flourished in Italy between the eighth and third centuries BCE. The Etruscan alphabet was modeled after the Greek alphabet. The Latin alphabet was a lot like the modern English alphabet, except it had only twenty-three letters. The missing letters were J, U, and W. Latin still had a U sound, but the letter V represented it.

MENSIS OCTOBER DIES·XXXI NONAE SEPTIMAN
MENSIS NOVEMBER DIES·XXX NON·QVINT DIES·HOR·VIIIS NOX·ITOR·XIIIS
MENSIS DECEMB DIES·XXXI NON·QVINT DIES·HOR·VIIII NOX·HOR·XV

This ancient Roman calendar illustrates the Latin alphabet's close resemblance to the English alphabet.

Roman Cursive

Roman scribes began writing in cursive around the first century CE. At first, Roman cursive was similar to the writing on Greek papyruses. Scribes sometimes connected words and characters with line strokes called ligatures.

Historians refer to the Romans' early style of longhand writing as Old Roman cursive. The Romans used this form of writing for about three hundred years. In the third century CE the style evolved into New Roman Cursive. Some letters in Old Roman cursive looked similar to modern capital letters. Those in New Roman cursive looked more like modern lowercase letters. New Roman cursive gradually developed into the cursive script used in English.

Bark and Beeswax

Papyrus was rare in parts of the Roman Empire. The Romans sometimes wrote on tree bark instead. They also wrote on very thin sheets of wood peeled from trees. But bark and wood dried out and rotted quickly. The Romans mainly used them for items that didn't have to last, such as to-do lists.

The Romans also wrote on wax tablets. Tabletmakers filled wooden frames with beeswax. People wrote in the wax with pointed wood, metal, or bone sticks. Wax tablets had holes in the edges so that several could be bound together. When the tablets were closed, the frames' raised edges protected the wax from damage.

Gaius's Gift

Soldiers sometimes took books from countries they defeated in battle. A Roman general named Lucius Licinius Lucullus built a huge home library of books he had taken from conquered lands. His library became a gathering place for famous Roman and Greek writers.

"Ingenia hominum rem publicam fecit [He made men's talents a public possession]."

—Pliny the Elder, Roman philosopher, on Gaius Asinius Pollio's public library, first century CE

A soldier and historian named Gaius Asinius Pollio constructed Rome's first public library around 40 BCE. It held thousands of Roman and Greek books. Roman rulers eventually built many other public libraries, partly to earn loyalty from their citizens.

Human Printing Presses

Books had to be copied by hand in ancient Rome. Book publishers realized it was inefficient for one person to copy one book. So they turned to readers and copyists. Many of these workers were enslaved.

To create multiple copies of books, a reader would slowly read a book to a room of copyists. The copyists would write each word, making many copies of a book at the same time. This method made books cheaper to produce. As books became cheaper, more people could buy them.

First Daily Newspaper

The first daily newspaper was probably Rome's Acta Diurna (Daily Events). Roman leader Julius Caesar started Acta Diurna in 59 BCE to inform citizens of government news and important events. But it also included human-interest items such as notices of births and deaths.

Government workers posted copies of the paper in public places so that many people could read them. Some wealthy people sent scribes to copy the paper for them to read and share at home.

Early Postal Systems

Many ancient civilizations developed postal systems for sending messages quickly over long distances. Rulers needed these systems to keep in touch with all parts of their empires.

Around 27 BCE, the Roman emperor Augustus developed an advanced postal system based on the similar

Time Savers

Abbreviations and acronyms make written communication simpler. The Romans developed hundreds of them. *SPQR*, for example, was short for *Senatus PopulusQue Romanus* (the senate and the people of Rome). The Romans used this abbreviation when talking about their government. *IMP* stood for *imperator*, the leader of the Roman army. Archaeologists have found Roman abbreviations on the surfaces of ancient coins and buildings.

Persian postal system. Roman couriers rode horses along Rome's roads. At first, they used a relay system where a courier would ride to a station and hand mail off to another courier. But the Romans later switched to a system where one courier carried the mail the whole way. If the person receiving the letter had any questions, the one courier was more likely to know the answer.

CONCLUSION
After the Ancients

Papermaking Spreads

After the Roman Empire fell to invaders in 476 CE, Europe entered a period called the Middle Ages (500–1500). Technology continued to spread during this time. Peoples outside China were beginning to learn about the Chinese method of making paper. Papermaking reached the areas of modern-day Korea and Japan in the 600s. In 751 the Chinese and Arab armies battled. The Arabs defeated the Chinese and took many prisoners, including papermakers. The Chinese papermakers showed them how to make paper.

The first paper mills were built in modern-day Iraq in the late 700s. Papermaking technology spread throughout the Middle East and into Spain. When European Christian armies fought against Muslim forces during the Crusades (1095–1291), European Christians also discovered Chinese papermaking methods and spread them further across Europe.

65

A Common Language

Even after the fall of the Roman Empire, Latin remained the common language of Europe. Many Europeans learned it in addition to their native language. Scholars, diplomats, and other leaders all used Latin for international relations.

The Renaissance began in Italy in the 1300s. Europeans took a renewed interest in learning, arts, and technology from the Classical period (700s BCE–400s CE). The Renaissance continued for several hundred years. Renaissance authors often wrote in Latin, especially when trying for an international audience. Latin remained the common language until the eighteenth century, when diplomats and scholars began using French.

A New Way to Print

German inventor Johannes Gutenberg played an important role in the explosion of knowledge during the Renaissance. He improved movable type and invented the modern printing press around 1450. Did Gutenberg know that the ancient Chinese invented printing presses several centuries earlier or even get his ideas from them? Historians can't say for sure.

Gutenberg's type was made from raised letters on equal-sized metal rectangles. They were easy to move, arrange into words, and lock in place. Then they could be removed and reused. His press was fast too. In 1452 Gutenberg printed his first book. It was a Latin version of the Bible. Gutenberg's model spread throughout the world. His printing press made books cheaper to produce and available to more people. It was one of the most important inventions in history.

The Rosetta Stone

In 1799 French soldiers fighting in Napoleon Bonaparte's army in Egypt discovered the key to decoding ancient Egyptian hieroglyphics. It was a slab of stone in the village of Rashid, which the French called Rosetta. The Rosetta Stone had three rows of the same text written in Greek, demotic, and hieroglyphic. Scholars translated the Greek words and later the demotic text. Between 1822 and 1824, French language expert Jean-François Champollion discovered how to translate the hieroglyphics. That allowed scientists to learn more about ancient Egyptian culture.

The Rosetta Stone unlocked mysteries of ancient Egypt when scholars translated the text carved on it. This replica of the stone shows the hieroglyphic (*top*), demotic (*middle*), and Greek (*bottom*) writing.

A System from Scratch

Most writing systems developed over hundreds of years, with hundreds of people adding, deleting, and changing words. But one man completed a writing system in only twelve years. Sequoyah was a member of North America's Cherokee Nation. He developed a syllabary for the Cherokee language.

Sequoyah started around 1809. By 1821 he had completed a syllabary with eighty-six symbols. He based some symbols on English letters, but his represented different sounds. The Cherokee Nation officially adopted the system in 1825.

Pictographs: Past to Present

Pictographs are all around us. Pictographs appear on the signs for public restrooms, emergency exits, and more. In the 1970s the US Department of Transportation made a list of fifty pictographs for airports and other places that travelers use. They provide information to people who can't read writing in an area's native language.

In 1972 the United States space program launched the probe Pioneer 10. The scientists attached a message to a plaque on the probe's antenna in case an extraterrestrial civilization ever found the spacecraft. Since aliens likely wouldn't understand any languages from Earth, the message was made up of pictures and symbols. It shows a female human and a male human. It also includes symbols to indicate the average human's size and Earth's location.

Then and Now

Think about the first cave paintings, alphabets, writing, parchment, and other ancient communication technologies. They may seem to have little in common with how we communicate. Modern communication technology includes smartphones, tablets, laptops, and more. Many people read and send dozens of digital messages each day. They communicate through the internet, not smoke signals. But modern communication technology owes its innovations to people who launched communication inventions thousands of years ago.

What do we need to send texts, direct messages, and emails? For most people in Europe and the Americas one answer is an alphabet developed 2,500 years ago in ancient Rome. Modern society could not function without the ancient invention of paper. Most digital books use a format introduced in ancient codices and books. Many modern typefaces have roots in ancient writing methods and the typefaces that were developed alongside early printing presses. Although ancient peoples could not have predicted the ways modern people would communicate, much of their culture has lasted through the ages.

TIMELINE

ca. 30,000 BCE	Ancient people paint in caves for the first time.
ca. 3100 BCE	Egyptian peoples learn how to make paper from papyrus.
3000s BCE	Mesopotamian writers begin scratching pictographic records on clay tablets.
3000s BCE	Chinese writers develop tapa for use as a writing surface.
3000s BCE	Egyptian peoples begin to write with hieroglyphics.
ca. 2800 BCE	Middle Eastern peoples begin to use pictures to stand for specific sounds.
1000s BCE	The Phoenicians adopt the North Semitic alphabet.
800s BCE	The Greeks adopt the Phoenician alphabet.
700s BCE	Egyptian scribes develop demotic writing.
600s BCE	The Romans adopt an alphabet from the Etruscans.
300s BCE	Ptolemy Soter begins to build the library of Alexandria in Egypt.
190 BCE	The Greeks develop parchment.
59 BCE	Roman leader Julius Caesar starts *Acta Diurna* (Daily Events), the world's first daily newspaper.
40 BCE	Roman historian Gaius Asinius Pollio constructs Rome's first public library.
27 BCE	Roman emperor Augustus develops an advanced postal system.
105 CE	Cai Lun creates paper from wood pulp.
100s	Chinese clothmakers develop block printing.
1000s	Chinese printers develop movable type.
1452	Johannes Gutenberg prints his first work with the modern printing press.

1800s	Indigenous peoples of the Great Plains refine Plains Indian Sign Language.
1821	Sequoyah completes the Cherokee language syllabary.
1990s	Archaeologists in San Lorenzo, Mexico, discover the Cascajal Block.
2011	The Dead Sea Scrolls are made available to view online.

GLOSSARY

abbreviation: a shortened form of a written word or phrase

acronym: a word formed from the first letters of words in a compound term

archaeologist: a scientist who studies the remains of past human cultures

artifact: a human-made object, especially one characteristic of a certain group or historical period

carbon dating: a process in which scientists estimate how old an organic material is by analyzing how much radiocarbon, an atom that decreases over time, that material still contains

cuneiform: a writing system developed in the ancient Middle East, consisting of wedge-shaped characters

cursive: a style of writing in which letters are connected by flowing lines

demotic: a simplified form of Egyptian hieratic writing

engraving: cutting lines or designs into a surface

extinct: no longer living

grammar: a system of rules about how to use a language

hieratic: a simplified form of Egyptian hieroglyphic writing

hieroglyphics: ancient Egyptian or Mayan picture-writing

ideogram: a picture or symbol that represents an object or idea

larynx: the voice box, which contains the vocal cords

logographic: written in symbols that represent words rather than sounds

mantra: spiritual sounds, words, or phrases that people repeat as a form of prayer

manuscript: a document in which text has been written rather than printed

ostraca: a stone used by the ancient Egyptians as a writing surface

papyrus: an Egyptian plant made into paper in ancient times; paper made from the papyrus plant

parchment: the skin of a sheep or goat made into a writing surface

phonogram: a symbol used to represent a sound

pictograph: a picture used for writing, sometimes also called a pictogram

printing: a technique for making identical copies of a document or image

prose: a style of writing close to ordinary spoken language

rhetoric: the art of writing or speaking effectively

syllabary: a set of written symbols representing spoken sounds from a language

typeface: all type of a single design, such as Times New Roman or Arial

verse: a style of writing common to poetry, featuring rhymes and repeated rhythms

SOURCE NOTES

25   "The nature of . . . for its memory.": Richard Parkinson and Stephen Quirke, *Papyrus* (Austin: University of Texas Press, 1995), 11.

41   "Set your heart . . . enjoy the arts.": Simon Leys, trans., *The Analects of Confucius* (New York: W.W. Norton and Company, 1997), 29.

62   "ingenia hominum rem . . . a public possession.": Edward Edwards, *Memoirs of Libraries: Including a Handbook of Liberal Economy* (London: Trubner, 1859), 34.

SELECTED BIBLIOGRAPHY

Adkins, Lesley, and Roy A. Adkins. *Handbook to Life in Ancient Rome*. New York: Facts on File, 1994.

Beshore, George. *Science in Ancient China*. New York: Franklin Watts, 1998.

Clark, Ronald W. *Works of Man*. New York: Viking, 1985.

Curtis, Gregory. *The Cave Painters: Probing the Mysteries of the World's First Artists*. New York: Anchor Books, 2007.

Hooker, J. T. *Reading the Past: Ancient Writing from Cuneiform to the Alphabet*. Berkeley, CA: University of California Press, 1990.

James, Peter, and Nick Thorpe. *Ancient Inventions*. New York: Ballantine Books, 1994.

Joseph, Frank, ed. *Discovering the Mysteries of Ancient America: Lost History and Legends, Unearthed and Explored*. Franklin Lakes, NJ: New Page Books, 2006.

Kirkpatrick, Nadia. *The Maya*. Chicago: Heinemann Library, 2003.

Martell, Hazel Mary. *Worlds of the Past: The Ancient Chinese*. New York: New Discovery Books, 1993.

Parkinson, Richard, and Stephen Quirke. *Papyrus*. Austin: University of Texas Press, 1995.

Robinson, Andrew. *The Story of Writing: Alphabets, Hieroglyphs and Pictograms*. New York: Thames and Hudson, 1995.

Saggs, H. W. F. *Civilization Before Greece and Rome*. New Haven, CT: Yale University Press, 1989.

Trumble, Kelly. *The Library of Alexandria*. New York: Clarion Books, 2003.

Walker, C. B. F. *Cuneiform*. Berkeley, CA: University of California Press, 1987.

Woods, Geraldine. *Science in Ancient Egypt*. New York: Franklin Watts, 1998.

FURTHER READING

Books

Bauser, Robin. *Fake News and Disinformation*. Buffalo: Rosen, 2023.
Social media and online news are some of the biggest
developments in communication technology. But they can also
make it easier to spread fake news. Starting with the invention of
the printing press, discover the history of news media and how to
combat disinformation.

Hoena, Blake. *Cell Phones and Smartphones: A Graphic History*.
Minneapolis: Graphic Universe, 2021.
The first telephone was patented in 1876. Since then, the invention
of cell phones and smartphones has transformed how people
connect and communicate, especially over long distances. Learn
about the history and modern advancements of phones.

Kamar, Haq. *The Evolution of Computer Technology*. New York:
Britannica Educational Publishing, 2019.
Early computers sometimes filled whole rooms. New computer
technology allows people to communicate, research, and more
with pocket-sized devices. Explore the development, evolution,
and importance of computer technology.

Woods, Michael and Mary B. Woods. *Computing through the Ages:
From Bones to Binary*. Minneapolis: Twenty-First Century
Books, 2024.
Throughout history, civilizations have used math to trade,
build, farm, and more. Learn about ancient computing systems
and how they evolved into modern numbers and math in this
historical primer.

Yenne, Bill. *100 Inventions that Shaped World History*. Naperville, IL:
Sourcebooks eXplore, 2023.
All modern technology has roots in earlier inventions and
advancements. From the printing press to virtual reality, this book
explores the history of technology through one hundred of the
most important discoveries and inventions.

Websites

American Printing History Association: History of Printing Timeline
https://printinghistory.org/timeline
Writing systems and the printing press revolutionized how
people accessed information. From the use of cuneiform to the
development of modern tablets and more, this in-depth timeline
examines the history of printing.

The Dead Sea Scrolls
https://www.deadseascrolls.org.il/?locale=en_US
The Leon Levy Dead Sea Scrolls Digital Library offers high-
resolution images of surviving Dead Sea Scroll fragments
alongside translations and historical explanations. Explore their
digital archive at this website.

Hand Papermaking: Beginner Series
https://www.handpapermaking.org/news-resources/beginner
-series
Check out this list of articles about handmade papermaking for
curious newcomers.

Lascaux: Visit the Cave
https://archeologie.culture.gouv.fr/lascaux/en/visit-cave
Take a virtual tour of ancient Lascaux cave art in France at this
webpage, hosted by the National Archaeological Museum in
France.

Penn Museum: Write Your Name in Cuneiform
http://www.penn.museum/cgi/cuneiform.php
This fun site lets visitors write their names and initials in
cuneiform on a virtual clay tablet.

INDEX

ABOUT THE AUTHORS

Michael Woods is a science and medical journalist in Washington, DC. He has won many national writing awards. Mary B. Woods is a school librarian. Their past books include the fifteen–volume *Disasters Up Close* series and many titles in the *Seven Wonders* series. The Woodses have four children. When not writing, reading, or enjoying their seven grandchildren, the Woodses travel to gather material for future books.

PHOTO ACKNOWLEDGMENTS

Image credits: JGI/Tom Grill/Getty Images, p. 5; Clement Philippe/Arterra Picture Library/Alamy, p. 7; Nando Rivero/Alamy, p. 9; Patrick Aventurier/Getty Images, p. 10; Eye Ubiquitous/Universal Images Group/Getty Images, p. 13; PeterHermesFurian/Getty Images, p. 15; Purchase, Raymond and Beverly Sackler Gift, 1988/Metropolitan Museum of Art p. 16; ESSAM AL-SUDANI/AFP via Getty Images, p. 17; Bert de Ruiter/Alamy, p. 18; De Agostini/Getty Images, p. 19; Zev Radovan/Alamy, p. 21; Fine Art Images/Heritage Images/Getty Images, p. 23; Getty Images, pp. 25, 34; duncan1890/Getty Images, p. 26; Gudella/Getty Images, p. 27; Alamy, pp. 28, 42, 56; Ann Ronan Pictures/Print Collector/Getty Images, p. 30; De Agostini/Getty Images, pp. 31, 61; joSon/Getty Images, p. 33; Artotop/Alamy, p. 38; B Christopher/Alamy, p. 39; Photo Lot 24 SPC Plains Dakota BAE 4722 00574500, National Anthropological Archives, Smithsonian Institution, p. 45; MPI/Getty Images, p. 45; Victor Cardoner/Getty Images, p. 47; Peter Horree/Alamy, p. 49; SL_Photography/Getty Images, p. 51; Wikimedia Commons PD, p. 52; M-Production/Getty Images, p. 55; PHAS/Universal Images Group/Getty Images, p. 56; Juan Naharro Gimenez/Getty Images, p. 67. Design elements: AnK_studio/Shutterstock; Ezhevika/Shutterstock.

Cover image: DEA/L. DE MASI/Getty Images